A Muslim is one who accepts

Allah as his creator,

And Muhammad as His Prophet,

And His beloved messenger.

A Muslim must be so sweet

Must be so sweet and kind.

He must not hurt anyone

And he must be colorblind.

A Muslim prays 5 times a day

As soon as she grows up.

She prays when the sun goes to sleep

And right before it wakes up.

She also prays when the sun stands up

In the middle of the day.

In the afternoon, and at sunset,

When yellow turns to gray.

A Muslim fasts every year

In the month of Ramadan.

For thirty days from dawn to dusk,

He must fast if he can.

And when you fast, you understand

Why hungry people cry.

You must try then to help them out,

Wipe the tears from their eyes.

A Muslim must give zakat,

Which means to help the poor.

She must give them every year

From what she saves and stores.

A Muslim must be generous

If he wants to blessed.

He must share from what he has

With those who have much less.

Once in his lifetime,

A Muslim must go on a pilgrimage.

He must visit Allah's house,

And perform his Hajj.

He must also go to Madina

And greet the Prophet.

But if he is ill or if he's poor,

He doesn't have to visit.

The greatest Muslim who ever lived

Is Prophet Muhammad.

Allah taught him everything

And so he was perfect.

A good Muslim is the one

Who follows his Prophet.

A good Muslim is the one

Who loves Muhammad.

Made in the USA
Lexington, KY
16 October 2017